MW01122387

ENOCH ARDEN
in the Hope Shelter

by Judith Thompson

based on Tennyson's "Enoch Arden"
and the melodrama for piano by Richard Strauss

160201

Enoch Arden in the Hope Shelter

by
Judith Thompson

based on Tennyson's "Enoch Arden" and the
melodrama for piano by Richard Strauss

Playwrights Canada Press
Toronto • Canada

Enoch Arden in the Hope Shelter © Copyright 2005 Judith Thompson
Introduction © Copyright 2006 Maria Lamont
The moral rights of the author are asserted.

Playwrights Canada Press
The Canadian Drama Publisher
215 Spadina Avenue, Suite 230, Toronto, Ontario CANADA M5T 2C7
416-703-0013   fax 416-408-3402
orders@playwrightscanada.com • www.playwrightscanada.com

Financial support provided by the taxpayers of Canada and Ontario through the Canada Council for the Arts and the Department of Canadian Heritage through the Book Publishing Industry Development Programme, and the Ontario Arts Council.

Front cover design by Kilby Smith-McGregor
Production Editor: JLArt

Library and Archives Canada Cataloguing in Publication

Thompson, Judith, 1954-
    Enoch Arden in the Hope Shelter / by Judith Thompson ; based on Tennyson's Enoch Arden and the melodrama for piano by Richard Strauss.

A play.
ISBN 0-88754-848-2

    I. Strauss, Richard, 1864-1949 II. Tennyson, Alfred Tennyson, Baron, 1809-1892. Enoch Arden III. Title.

PS8589.H4883E56 2006   C812'.54   C2006-905430-4

First edition: October 2006.
Printed and bound by Canadian Printco at Scarborough, Canada.

Acknowledgements

Richard Strauss "Enoch Arden"
© Robert Forberg Musikverlag, by permission of G. Ricordi &
Co.
München

"Morgen!"
Music by Richard Strauss
Lyrics adapted from poems by John Henry Mackay
Edited by Laura Ward and Richard Walters
Copyright © 1995 by Hal Leonard Corporation
International Copyright Secured. All Rights Reserved.

This play is for Sophia

Table of Contents

Introduction

Prima la Musica

Today the word "melodrama" instantly connotes visions of villains and heroines from the 19th century's painted scenery traditions. However, the Greek meaning of the word translates to literally the combination of "music" and "acting." Granted, there may be a shared quality of heightened emotion in both "melodramas," but there the similarities of this musical genre and its theatrical soap opera cousin end. The melodrama form is a musical technique which combines music and spoken text or poetry. The two art forms work together in a way that emphasizes the emotional through-line of a work or dramatic moment. The technique has appeared in classical western music for centuries, and even Mozart pondered if it wasn't the perfect way to combine two art forms. "It is not sung, but only declaimed, and the music is like an *obbligato recitative*," he wrote to his father in 1778, "Occasionally there is also speech underneath the music, which makes a marvellous effect." Unfortunately, Mozart's own attempt at the genre was limited to his incomplete opera *Zaide*—he never finished a more evolved attempt at the form in his short life. However, the melodrama form continued to develop along the fringes of the operatic and classical music repertoire, ultimately achieving a peak of popularity in the Romantic and Late Romantic period. Its intimate style lent itself particularly well to the parlours and small salon concerts of the time. Many composers tried their hands at melodramas, either as an independent art form (Benda, R. Strauss, Rousseau, Lizst, Nietzche), or for dramatic effect in a larger musical work, for example the grave-digging scene which precedes the climax of Beethoven's only opera *Fidelio*. Other notable examples include J. Strauss's operetta *Die Fledermaus*, Weber's *Der Freischutz*, and the prologue of Berg's *Lulu*. In the twentieth century, the melodrama form was employed to masterly effect by Schoenberg in his *tour de force* for performer and chamber orchestra, *Pierrot Lunaire*, an evolution of the technique which the composer described as "speech melody." Surely film and television scores represent the modern apogee of the melodrama form, where it is impossible to imagine seeing any movie or television drama without music or soundscape underlying the dialogue.

Richard Strauss was a young up-and-coming composer when he tried his hand at the melodrama form with *Enoch Arden*. *Enoch* was his opus 38, written in 1897 when Strauss was 33. Many consider it one of the best examples of the melodrama genre of that period. Alfred Lord Tennyson's 1864 epic poem "Enoch Arden" was one of the Poet Laureate's most beloved and popular works both in Britain and in Germany. It received several translations into German in the intervening thirty years before Strauss took it as the source for his foray into the melodrama form. Throughout Strauss's problematic career path, ambition drove him (often blindly) to find success and an audience for his work at any cost. Even the creation of this very early work, which essentially brought him his first widespread success, demonstrates his cool career tactics. In later years, Strauss dismissed the work, in part because of his motives in writing it— to curry favour with its dedicatee and original performer, the General Director of the Munich State Opera, Ernst Von Possart. *Enoch Arden* was a huge popular success for Strauss, and brought a surge of attention to the young composer. He and Von Possart made several tours performing the work together (Strauss at the piano) to sold-out audiences throughout Europe. It was still to be another ten years until Strauss achieved his first true operatic triumph with *Salome* (this time to a text of Oscar Wilde), and cemented his position in the firmament of twentieth century composers. *Enoch Arden* has retained its position along the fringes of the repertoire of the last century because of its inventive manipulation of the melodrama form and its virtuosic solo piano passages.

Poi le parole...

When I began investigating melodramas in search of an intimate classical work to stage, I was struck by the musical tenderness and evocative moods in many passages of Strauss's *Enoch Arden*. It is a rarely performed work by one of the twentieth century's greatest musical and operatic masters; as well, it is one of only one or two works for solo piano Strauss composed in his lifetime. I became convinced that this work could still speak to a modern audience, but not necessarily in its existing form. Thus, the tiny germ for *Enoch Arden in the Hope Shelter* was born. I felt the time for a theatrical re-examination of the melodrama form was ripe, but only with the aid of a very astute and talented adaptor, who could have the courage and flair to completely break the piece open and put it together again. I approached Judith Thompson to write a modern adaptation of the work for the following reasons: because I know her to be artistically fearless, as well as a generous collaborator, but chiefly because I feel her writing is among the most musical and poetic of any living playwright working today in the English language. We entered the process in the spirit of an exploratory workshop in the summer of 2003 (funded by the Canada Council for the Arts) with no production goal in mind. Rather, we wanted to see if it was even possible to create a modern piece of theatre out of this 100-year-old work. The only theatrical constraint I asked of Judith was to have the pianist play a character in the play, somehow based on the role of Annie Lee in the poem, thus a work for one male actor and a female musician. After several days of reading and playing through the source material of Strauss's melodrama, Judith came in to rehearsals one day with the narrative key for a new work: the story of two mental patients (or "consumers of psychiatric services") living in a halfway house in Toronto's Parkdale. A kind of story within a story, the characters would perform scenes and parts of the melodrama, relating the experiences of Tennyson's love triangle to events in their own lives. One character speaks in great chunks of virtuosic verbal mania, the other mute in language but capable of deep expression through her playing and singing.

The creation process was spread out over the better part of two years in small workshops (like the 2004 Tarragon Spring Arts Fair, as well as a presentation at the 2004 Summerworks Festival in Toronto). Throughout that time, many details of the narrative and story changed and evolved, but the seed of Judith's idea only grew in strength. It proved to be an enormously joyful and rewarding experience for all the artists involved. I felt honoured to watch Judith's process at such close range, to witness her immense craftsmanship and her sheer technical brilliance as she worked her way through each draft, creating large portions of the drama spontaneously in the rehearsal hall. The mood in the workshop process was a generous one, with much conversation, storytelling, and laughter. Judith is sometimes informed by details from the performer's personalities. For example, John Fitzgerald Jay, who played Jabber, is an actor originally from Halifax, as is Thompson's husband Gregor Campbell. The connection between Canada's East and Tennyson's sleepy British fishing village seemed a natural one. At times during performances, I felt that *Enoch* was Judith's love letter to the East Coast of Canada. A turning point in the development of *Enoch* occurred during the second series of rehearsals preceding the Summerworks creation in 2005. I had hired a young musician Kristin Mueller, who happened not only to play the piano beautifully, but was also an accomplished classical singer and talented improviser. Kristin dramatically affected the growth of the piece, since her singing and musical knowledge gave us much more freedom in exploring the melodrama form. Ultimately, what was most rewarding was the feeling of re-inventing the melodrama form—where the original Strauss music did not fit a new mood or feeling in Judith's text or story, we searched for musical expression in other ways, whether through Kristin's improvisation, a waltz by Johann Strauss, or a *Lied* by Richard Strauss.

The rehearsal process always provokes stories, tales, and sharing. In the many conversations during the creation process, Judith spoke frequently of the de-institutionalization of the mental-healthcare system by the Ontario Government during the 1980s. In no small way is this event connected to the world of Jabber and Ciel, and to the world of the urban streets which has confronted Toronto citizens over the last 15 years—the homelessness, the lack of care, the poverty, and the clear lack of a system of support for those suffering from mental illness. We were once more confronted by the timeliness of this story when final rehearsals took place at the new Theatre Centre facility, which is the direct neighbour of the Queen Street Institute for Mental Health in Parkdale. It seemed right that *Enoch Arden* should take place there.

Judith Thompson's writing is fuelled by her passionate sense of justice and her strong social conscience. All of her characters struggle to communicate their deepest inner longings to be heard, to be understood, to be witnessed. Most of them pitch themselves against immense injustices to express themselves. There were no overt political motives on Thompson's part in the creation of Jabber and Ciel. Like all her characters, they spring unbidden from the deepest parts of her unconscious, unchecked, and somehow whole. Like a verbal Michelangelo, Thompson slowly carves away the excess to reveal what always existed in the depths of her imagination.

I am deeply grateful to Judith, John, and Kristin and all the artists who participated in the creation of *Enoch Arden*. I am also indebted to Franco Boni, Artistic Director of the Theatre Centre, whose belief in this work made it all possible.

—Maria Lamont, Director

Enoch Arden in the Hope Shelter was first produced under the name *Enoch Arden by Alfred, Lord Jabber and his Catatonic Songstress* by the Theatre Centre, Toronto, in September 2005, with the following company:

JABBER   John Fitzgerald Jay
CIEL   Kristin Mueller

Artistic Director: Franco Boni

Directed by Maria Lamont
Music by Richard Strauss
Set and lighting design by David Skelton
Costume design by Erin Haid

Characters

Ciel
Jabber

A Note About the Music

Most music references are laid out as follows: 31/5/1. The first number represents the page number in this book, the second number refers to the line on the page, and the third number represents the bar number. So in this case it would be page 31, line 5, bar 1.

Acknowledgements

I would like to thank Maria Lamont, for asking me to adapt Tennyson's great epic poem "Enoch Arden," and giving me the freedom to do what I wanted with it. Maria's extraordinary understanding of Strauss's music and Tennyson's text was of immeasurable value in creating *Enoch Arden in the Hope Shelter*, and her fine instincts as a director gave the play a wonderful first production.

I am also deeply grateful to Kristen Mueller and John Fitzgerald Jay, for their brilliance in interpreting and premiering these roles, and to Franco Boni for producing this show, both at Summerworks and at the late Theatre Centre.

Enoch Arden
in the Hope Shelter

CIEL, a beautiful and wild looking woman with profound depression, who has spent a lifetime in and out of institutions, stands in the dark with only the light of the moon on her face staring out of the window. She is in a catatonic state triggered by the death of her infant, several months before.

We hear a recording of the noises inside her head. Prelude Music (p.30).

JABBER, a psychotic, sometimes homeless, man who is dressed in a ragged dressing gown sits and stares at CIEL.

JABBER   Ciel? Cieel? Ciel? Ciel? Ciel? Come on now, you're scaring me, are you there? Hey, you know the talent show is two days away Ciel; *(a piano scale plays tentatively in her head)* two days till showtime and and and I been telling EVERYONE we are gonna win they got a pool goin it's a big prize, Ciel, a BIG BIG prize we gotta chance to climb outa this shitpit life we're living come on Ciel aren't you sick of living with crackheads and crazies in this halfway house in this skanky part of Parkdale? We're not like them we come from WAY up the ladder you and me I was linguistically lubriciously on my way to something and and you, well oh my Henry! You were a famous singing mouse or something like that. Are you gonna just TOSS away all that hard work we have done? All those happy play practices you used to be so smiley and happy you would play your music with your very French northeast of the Gaspe buttertarts and tourtière love and look at ya now, you're a sad sack, a sack of potatoes, just another suicidally surrendered psychiatric sickee. I mean if ya keep going like this you're gonna be dead and I can't bring someone back from the dead. There is only one person who can bring someone back from the dead and that is Dwayne Moncreif of Sault Ste. Marie who has now actually been deposed and is washing dishes at the Tim Horton's all because of what Diane Cable told everybody but that is neither here nor there. So Ciel, how about playing the music for our story, maybe right now, maybe the music that we were working on for the talent show before you started playing statue, how about we start working on that again again, like say in one minute minus 15 seconds or so? Come on, we can show 'em that their Kraft

Kristin Mueller, John Fitzgerald Jay
photo by R. Kelly Clipperton

Dinners and bedbugs and couches smelling of pee are not getting us down! We are SHOWPEOPLE there's NO people like SHOW people…. Now Ciel we gotta start working on it now, *MAINTENANT*. Bernie's doing a hip-hop dance, Josephine's singing her country songs, we got stiff competition! Come on, come on.

We used to be buddies, didn't we? Friends forever. You would tell me everything, you would tell me when your period came and how many teaspoons of sugar ya had in your *café au lait* and if your bum was itchy…

And and that you stole Penny's Swiss Army knife and now you won't even look at me. Jesus Murphy and Josephine. Enough already BORE ME TO DEATH BABY! I know I know I know you are blue and a little depressed, but we got a talent show coming up here, and you and me are gonna win the winner gets a free pass to Wonderland, Ciel, and VIP coupons for a movie, and a Tim Hortons's hat, and a free doughnut, and a Big Harv from Harvey's and a future.

A future that is not a dead end life livin on disability in a Parkdale mental house CIEL. Did you hear what I said before? Look at Maurice out there, he's been sitting in that chair for 12 years for God's sake, you wanna go like Maurice? A big drooling nothing,

pooping in his diapers and bein spoonfed applesauce? I'll get you
a ferret, Shane has one, he'll give it to me if I give him a blow job.

Oh. Right. Okay. Okay, Ciel. Ciel. Ciel. Do you see what I see? I know
you don't like me to say it out loud, but I can't help but notice.
They're gone. They're gone. You've done it, with your standing
and your staring you've saved the world you superstar, you veered
them away from our planet, you've done it again. Look, there's not
a demon in sight! *(He shouts at the demons.)* And don't you come
back here ever ever, hear me ya fugnuts? Ya red devils? See? See? It's
clear. It's okay now. Parkdale is safe. We're gonna be okay Ciel. And
I thank you for saving us once again. Oh my Ciel…

> *CIEL begins to walk slowly toward the piano. She hears the*
> *music in her head.*

I would do anything for you *mon angèle*. I would lay down my life
for you I would lay on the ground, I would steal the Pentagon,
Parliament Hill, Wayne Gretsky's hat, I would become a snail, a sick
dragon, an accountant—actually I did pass the actuarial exams with
flying colours, could have been an actuary ask my aunt, she was
CRUSHED when I chose to live my life—as a psychotic. That's why
she donated her piano to the halfway house here, half way to what
I don't know—hoping it would give me focus—my God if she could
see it now she would turn in her grave though she doesn't necessarily
die till next week.

> *CIEL plays p.31 Andante, repeating 31/1/1-31/3/1*
> *as necessary. JABBER speaks over the music.*

ENOCH ARDEN by Alfred Lord Tennyson.

Long lines of cliff breaking
have left
a chasm;
And in the chasm are foam and yellow sands

> *CIEL continues to play as above, increasing the tempo, getting*
> *into the story, sometimes making small mistakes with the*
> *playing.*

See, see I didn't tell you this before but the poem, it's about my DAD
who actually did come back from the dead and it stars me, the sickly
child, AND the kind suitor, I play two characters actually, and of
course you, the angelical Annie Lee, and the nuns in St. John the

Sacred Heart of Jesus made us memorize the goddamned thing—
they beat me with a stick until I got every word but I did I got every
word right—I worked on it for 12 days and nights every minute of
every day. Tuesday Ciel, Tuesday night, 6:45 over at the Parkdale
Community Centre by the Church of the Holy Martyrs.

Yes, Sister Michael John breaking heart of Jesus Kristy I know every
word! At least I think I know every word, I used to know every
word, now what is that phrase after "yellow sands" something like—
something like...

Here it is coming to me like a wave like a wave waving...

Long lines of cliff breaking
have left
a chasm;
And in the chasm are foam and yellow sands

Look! Look! oh my Henry, look at that Ciel. I can't believe it, it's
exactly like where I grew up it's EERIE.

It makes me all shaky, it's making my eyes water, oh my yes!

Beyond, RED ROOFS about a narrow wharf
In cluster; then a moulder'd church; and higher
A long street climbs to one tall-tower'd mill

> *CIEL plays music as above, but this time only the right hand*
> *chord pattern of Andante, repeated.*

That's where I'm from Ciel I'll take ya there there when this is over,
bus leaves Bay street for St. John at 11:30 every Thursday. You and
me we will get on that bus and go visit my aunt Arthena. She'll just
be sittin there waiting for me she'll give us tea and say "how are you
enjoying my grand piano?"

That's exactly like our little place on the Chedabuctoo you wouldn't
BELIEVE how this is like he has BEEN there. Course he was there,

And high in heaven behind it a gray down
With Danish barrows; and a hazelwood,
By autumn nutters haunted

Have you ever been nutting? I'll take you it's a blast, ya pick up *les*
petites noisettes and put em in a pie,

Here on this beach a hundred years ago,
Three children of three houses

> *Attaca music into Allegretto section p.31.*

Annie Lee, that's you, Ciel, that's you she's just like you perfectitious like you, princess in the pea, just like you.

> *CIEL stops playing. Looks at JABBER.*

In fact,

I don't know. I believe in other lives, do you? I believe that that that that you see, this is my story. And your story, soon as I saw it in this mouldy old book they keep in the common room, soon as I read it, a DAM broke open and my memory exploded, see fact is,

I told this to him. I told this to Alfred, sitting in a bar, yeah, Alfred LORD Tennyson you betcha see he was over here, he was fascinated by the colonies, and and he accosted me, asked me to show him a moose, or a beaver or persons native to this land or or a typical lumberjack bar and and so we got to talking and I told him,

MY STORY and here it is, in print, he stole it from me shamelessly and then barrelled it back a few hundred years Ciel, and he got famous for it, before before, and he is studied now, and making royalties offa my story oh his cousins in the sky aren't *(gibberish)* and it PISSES ME OFF.

'Cause I lived through it, Ciel, I suffered through it and SO DID YOU. Stop hunchin your shoulders like that Ciel! That's always a sign you're going back in, don't go back in. Catatonia is not becoming it's frankly annoying; last time you stood in one position for 12 days, ya hardly peed, you were green, I kept explaining to everyone you are not turning to stone you are protecting us from pre-historic perambulating pernicious predators, so let's continue our play story NOW because time is ticking, hear it? Hear it? And we gotta be on that stage together at the Community Centre at 6:45 in front of 20-30 people, Ciel, I can't go on alone, I'll be too embarrassed, see, we gotta gotta do this so so, I know why, so that the people out there look at us with respect, just because we walk around with our pyjamas on, and and slippers, and just because we we seem to be talking to nobody, or our hair isn't nicely brushed they think we are low, low forms of life but when they hear your beautiful music when they hear this olden days poem this epic epic of epicness they will see we are keeping the world from—

> *CIEL starts playing Allegretto section p.31 again, pulling him back into the music.*

Here on this beach a hundred years ago,
Three children of three houses, Annie Lee,
and Philip Ray the miller's only son so he is filthy rich just like me,
I gotta trust fund, my mum discovered Pop Tarts, did you know
that? *And Enoch Arden, a rough sailor's lad Made orphan by a winter*
shipwreck, play'd Among the waste and lumber of the shore

So you remember, 5000 years ago the three of us played. 'Member we played house in the narrow cave that ran beneath the cliff—And one day Enoch would be your husband and the next day me:

but at times Enoch would hold possession for a week:
"This is my house and this my little wife."
"Mine too" said Philip "turn and turn about:"
When, if they quarrell'd, Enoch stronger-made
Was master: then would Philip, his blue eyes
All flooded with the helpless wrath of tears,
Shriek out "I hate you, Enoch"

> *CIEL plays 32/2/1 (the first chord coincides with "hate"*
> *above), through until end of p.32, with a repeat of 32/4/2 if*
> *extra time is needed.*

Because oh my God the guy was massive, and scary, and he would kick me in the stomach and you, always the peacemaker, you would say "shutup—I love you both."

'Cause that's the kind of girlie you are.

'Cause you are the peacemaker, the dove, the pretty piano player, the porridge maker, the peerless procrastinator, the palliator, the permeator, the silent, silent, for 4 1/2 months silent...

> *Music ends.*

Like an angel.

> *CIEL begins to play again 33/1/1 – 33/2/2, repeating as*
> *needed (two times at least).*

But when the dawn of rosy childhood past,
And the new warmth of life's ascending sun
Was felt by either, either fixt his heart
On that one girl

But Enoch, the bastard, he told you explicitly, he looked at you and said "I love you" and me, I just couldn't. I was unable. You know I'm shy as a bird.

> CIEL *repeats music 33/1/1 – 33/1/3,* JABBER *speaks over the last of the music.*

A carefuller in peril, did not breathe
Than Enoch.
he thrice had pluck'd a life
From the dread sweep of the down-streaming seas

Well Enoch he saved up his money, he bought a boat and a sweet little house, you know he did, but Philip, he is lovin ya, thinking maybe JUST MAYBE he has a hair of a chance.

> CIEL *plays music Allegro moderato (the "nutting" music)* 33/3/1 *until end of p.34,* JABBER *speaks over the music.*

Then, on a golden autumn eventide,
The younger people making holiday,

With bag and sack and basket, great and small, Went nutting to the hazels. Me, I stayed home, my dad was sick eh, he's lost both his legs from diabetes and one was going gangrenous so I left later, eh, but when Dad passed off to sleep, I ran, I ran till I was puking up up the pretty mountain, catchin up with the happy nutters *as he climb'd the hill, Just where the prone edge of the wood began To feather toward the hollow, saw the pair,*

Enoch and Ciel, the two of ya, sittin hand in hand, *His large gray eyes and weather-beaten face All-kindled by a still and sacred fire,* that'd be "I love you" love, *That burn'd as on an altar.* I looked, *And in their eyes and faces read* my *doom;* When I saw you and Francis in the laundry room, inside all those white sheets, naked, inside all those white sheets, I went off like a wounded mole, and while the rest of you were merry making, *Had my dark hour unseen, and rose and past Bearing a lifelong hunger in* my *heart.*

CIEL finishes playing the last section on p.34. Pause. JABBER
then continues.

For you, Ciel. For your silent silentness, I mean other women speak
like a crowd of crows *(He makes crow sounds.)* you speak with your
music.

And and and and your music, lets me speak.

That other language I speak out in the halls and in the cafeteria?

Lugiangeouengoughe ghe rrthows; showuhs!!! *(gibberish scenario)*

That language? That's just to throw em off, so they won't talk to me.
You are the only one I speak English with.

CIEL plays wedding music—an improvisation on Purcell's
"Trumpet Voluntary."

So Enoch and Annie *were wed, and merrily rang the bells,*
And the bridesmaids are in turquoise and tangerine
And ya got Vince Pottie's one-man band, Junie Morrison's seafood
castle, and my own date squares.
And merrily ran the years, seven happy years,
And I'm just a dinky donkey friend that comes over to play cribbage
and hear how honking happy the two of youse are.

CIEL plays 3 lines of the first movement of Mozart's "Sonata
K.331" transposed into G major.

first a daughter. In him woke,
With his first babe's first cry, the noble wish
To save all earnings to the uttermost,
And give his child a better bringing-up
Than his had been, or hers;
a wish renew'd,

When two years after came a boy to be
The rosy idol of her solitudes,
While Enoch was abroad on wrathful seas,

Then came a change, as all things human change.
Enoch clambering on a mast in harbor, Ten miles to northward of the
narrow port *by mischance he slipt and fell—*

CIEL plays a dissonant chord.

John Fitzgerald Jay
photo by R. Kelly Clipperton

That accident when he broke his leg down in Yarmouth and he can't get home and he is staying at his aunt Rosalie, and then while he's lying there with his leg broke, *his* good *wife* Annie, still in the narrow port, *Bore him another son, (CIEL plays an improvisation on Mozart's Sonata K.331. First movement, transposed to G minor, approximately 4 bars) a sickly one.* Well he can't stand this, knowing his wife and baby are ten miles away, so he hobbles right back, ten long miles in agonizing paralyzing pain, over hill and dale and cobblestone. Of course he did, he wanted to be with his wife and baby, who wouldn't? But then after the inexpressible joy of kissing his new tiny lad and beauteous wife, things went down and down.

Another hand crept too across his trade Taking her bread and theirs:
and on him fell, doubt and gloom.
He seem'd, as in a nightmare of the night,
To see his children leading evermore
Low miserable lives of hand-to-mouth,

So Rosalie she worried sick he's gonna jump offa the pier so she tells her boyfriend's brother-in-law Mike Noseworthy who's sailing out to China to pick up wicker baskets and tiger paws and that, a big load for Montreal, for all them little bamboo shops, right? And he says for sure, if he knows his way around a boat, we need him.

Enoch says: "I'm there baby, sign me up, Hallelujah we are gonna be rich!"

Well, I remember like it was yesterday when he come home, and you're trying to nurse your little one, who's fussy as all get out, a feeble infant, but oh some cute, and I was there, havin a cup of tea with ya, and when he says he's goin to China you just about lost it. 'Member? You look at me and I don't know what to say it's none of my business, and I'm looking at the floor, and you *Besought him, supplicating,* but Enoch he made up his mind.

So he sets you up in a tea shop that he built himself,

So all day long till Enoch's last at home,
Shaking their pretty cabin, hammer and axe,
Auger and saw, while Annie seem'd to hear
Her own death-scaffold raising

She was scared silly but she loved her tea, they got the Darjeeling, the Earl Grey, the Lapsang Suchong, and your herbal tea, rosehips plucked right from the bushes, you like rosehip remember? Rosehip jam, and melted butter on a nice hot hunka bread? You know? *(She looks depressed.)* Hey. Hey, Ciel, you know you are—I never had so much fun putting on a show with anybody—not the King of Spain or Mr Dressup or even Jesus of Nazereth, they were snoring boring compared to you, your music? Makes me shiver.

SO. ANY old way ya liked making the tea and the tasty tea cakes for your customers, sure, she enjoyed that in a way, but all the while she never smiled, kinda like, something like you Ciel. She never smiled because she lived in dread, in deepest dread of that day she knew would surely come.

> *CIEL plays reprise of 34/3/4 through until bottom of p.34,*
> *JABBER speaks over the music.*

So one day Enoch walks in, sexy as hell, sees her crying in her tea, he takes her by the little hand and says:
"My *Annie, this voyage by the grace of God*
Will bring fair weather yet to all of us.
Keep a clean hearth and a clear fire for me,
For I'll be back, my girl, before you know it"
Then lightly rocking baby's cradle "and he,
This pretty puny weakly little one,—
Nay, for I love him all the better for it—
God bless him, he shall sit upon my knees
And I will tell him tales of foreign parts,
And make him merry, when I come home again.
Come Annie, come, cheer up before I go."

At length she said,

> *CIEL plays 35/1/1 – 35/1/8 and sings with the chords:*

CIEL
"*O Enoch you are wise;*
And yet for all your wisdom well know I
That I shall look upon your face no more."

> *JABBER waits until the music finishes, then continues.*

JABBER
And Enoch he replies, he says, "*Cast all your cares on God; that anchor holds. Is He not yonder in those uttermost Parts of the morning? if I flee to these Can I go from Him? and the sea is His, The sea is His: He made it.*"

That is STRAIGHT from the BIBLE and it is my prayer.
IS HE NOT YONDER IN THOSE UTTERMOST Parts of morning?

He is Ciel, oh he is,
So Enoch he gives ya a kiss and squeezes the little ones and he shakes my hand and and

And you give him a curl of the baby's hair.

A CURL of the BABY'S HAIR. You know, to remember the baby by so he will never forget the sad and puny and blessed baby and so she stands on the pier with the 3 darling little ones, saying goodbye and her beloved Enoch sails away Away and away till she sees him no more and she takes the kids back home up the narrow wharf and the cobbled streets and life goes on…

and winter turns to spring and spring turns into summer, and summer into fall, and fall into winter, January into February, February into March,

> CIEL plays p.35, Allegro Appassionato. JABBER continues, muttering under the music.

And that made one whole year, that's 12 months, that's 52 weeks, 365 days, 24 hours in a day, 60 minutes in an hour, 60 seconds in a minute,

And your tea shop is not doing well, the cookies are stale the tea is like dishwater you are just too sad to care! And the baby is not doing well neither. *(CIEL's playing peters out, ending approximately 36/2/1.)*

I'm telling ya, weak as a gutter kitten he just kept getting worse, coughin, sleepin, sleepin all the time, wouldn't take your milk, no matter what you done and my theory is that is why you stopped talking cause you you blames yourself; the poor little thing clearly had a weak heart, Ciel, you were doing everything right; you were breastfeedin him with your very own breast milk all white and creamy you were burping him, ya quit smoking crack, you were changing him when he was wet, you were a good mother. You were always lovin up that little guy. He just stopped breathing on account of his delicate heart. It's something that happens sometimes. There wasn't nothing you coulda done.

THERE WASN'T NOTHIN YOU COULDA DONE DIFFERENT.

> CIEL plays 36/2/2 until approximately 36/4/1.

After a lingering,—ere she was aware,—
Like the caged bird escaping suddenly,
The little innocent soul flitted away.

> *CIEL plays music p.37 Agitato. CIEL walks away from the*
> *piano.*

Well that funeral was the saddest thing I ever seen
About fourteen people.
Rainy cold day.
Tiny little coffin the size of a shoebox.

I come to see you after, you know, look in on you,
You are remembering Ciel, aren't ya?
I can see a flicker. A flicker a flutter
I come in the door. No sound, nothing. The kids are in school, or at
your sister's, whatever.
You are just sittin. Just like you have done for the last 12 days, just
sitting and staring and turning into stone or cement,

So I, me, Phillip, sit down
And I say "Annie I got a proposal
No not that kind of proposal just look, I'm rich, I got money, Dad
owns the mill for God's in heavens sake let me pay for the kids'
clothes and dentist."

"And it would vex Enoch *even in his grave,*
If he could know his babes were running wild
Like colts about the waste. So Annie, now—
Have we not known each other all our lives?"

Do me a favour. It would be a favour to me.

Then Annie with her brows against the wall
Answer'd

CIEL   *(sings) "I cannot look you in the face;*
I seem so foolish and so broken down.
When you came in my sorrow broke me down; And now I think your
kindness breaks me down;"

JABBER   Remember? Remember the look on my face?

So everything is going quite smooth as far as I'm concerned, kids are
happy, you are actually smiling from time to time throw me a word
or two, the kids are calling me Father Philip.

CIEL plays p.36, Moderato—36/4/1 until the end of the page.

Philip gain'd As Enoch lost; for Enoch seem'd to them Uncertain as a vision or a dream, Faint as a figure seen in early dawn Down at the far end of an avenue, Going we know not where:

CIEL plays the A minor variation of Mozart's Sonata K.331 (without repeats). JABBER continues after the music finishes.

And so you know how it goes so fast so slow day after day, month after month and TEN YEARS PASS I don't know how it happened, season into season, kids are grown, my hair is graying and NOT a WORD from Enoch well I figured he had hooked up with a beauty from the South Seas Islands and was just livin the Life of Reilly, you know, lyin in a hammock drinking from a cracked up coconut, bein fanned with the fronds of a palm tree, dancing girls all round, big red flowers, like many men before him, he just disappeared into the horizon so what's new, right?

Ciel plays p.33, Allegro moderato "nutting" music—33/3/1 until approximately 33/5/4.

Well, meanwhile back back at home, it's autumn and another nutting time again and and me and you, we are blissed man we are pickin the hazelnuts outa the trees the ones the squirrels haven't already got and we sit down, soft grass

and I go, *"Annie, it is beyond all hope, against all chance, That he who left you ten long years ago Should still be living; well then—let me speak: I grieve to see you poor and wanting help: I cannot help you as I wish to do Unless—they say that women are so quick—Perhaps you know what I would have you know—I wish you for my wife."*

Then answer'd Annie; tenderly she spoke:

CIEL *(sings with chords based on 45/4/1, beat 2 – 45/5/1, beat 3)* "You have been as God's good angel in our house."

JABBER That's like me Ciel, walkin you to your electroshock, holding your hand when you're in your trances, screamin at the nurses when they tell you you haven't gone pee in 12 hours, that's none of their blasted ass business—and you go

CIEL *(sings)* "Can one live twice? can you be ever loved As Enoch was?"

JABBER *"I am content"* he answer'd *"to be loved A little after Enoch."* Get it? Get it Ciel? That's my way of saying that I don't mind gettin the leftovers—I am happy to be second, even third on your list oh oh oh so this next part KILLS me, okay so she tells him just in case Enoch returns to us—

CIEL   (*sings with chords 45/5/1, beat 1 & beat 3*) "Let's wait a year."

JABBER   —he is CRESTFALLEN but he's a gentleman so he goes "very well, very well, Ciel a year it is but not a day MORE you have to marry me in a year." Well, she looks at the ground, he takes off, he's thinking about it behind *the dead flame of the fallen day* and he runs back to her and he goes *"I was wrong.* You don't owe me nothing. You don't have to marry me when a year is up or ever, that was in *your hour of weakness. I am always bound to you, but you are free."*

CIEL   (*sings with chords based on 45/6/2 – 45/6/4*) "I am bound."

> *JABBER and CIEL dance to a recorded time waltz ("Tales from the Vienna Wood" by J. Strauss), then JABBER continues alone as CIEL plays over the music. At the end of the waltz, CIEL segues into p.33 "nutting" music—33/3/1 until 33/3/5 (transposed into F major).*

JABBER   Then *autumn into autumn flash'd again, And there* Philip *stood once more before her face,*

CIEL   (*sings*) "Is it a year?"

JABBER   She wasn't really ready, *So much to look to—such a change— Then Philip with his eyes Full of that lifelong hunger, and his voice Shaking a little like a drunkard's hand, "Take your own time, Annie, take your own time."* But *the lazy gossips of the port, Abhorrent of a calculation crost, Began to chafe as at a personal wrong.*

Everybody is talking from Peggy's Cove to Lunenburg yakety yak *And one,* Diane Cable *in whom all evil fancies clung Like serpent eggs together, laughingly would hint* oh I won't even say what she was hinting at, it was ugly as my grandmother's bed sores, well the kids were pressing Annie "come on, marry the guy, we love Father Philip" well she is puttin it off and puttin it off *At last one night it chanced that Annie could not sleep,*

> *CIEL plays p.39 ("Annie's Dream")—plays to bottom of page, repeating the last 4 bars as necessary. JABBER speaks over the music.*

but earnestly Pray'd for a sign

CIEL (*pauses in her playing and sings*) *"my Enoch is he gone?"*

> *CIEL resumes playing.*

JABBER *Then compass'd round by the blind wall of night Brook'd not the expectant terror of her heart,*

> *Started from bed, and struck herself a light, Then desperately seized the holy Book, Suddenly set it wide to find a sign, Suddenly put her finger on the text*—my mum does that, and all my aunts and uncles, in times of trouble they say "Jabber, get me my Bible, and open it" because they think I'm touched, eh, with divine madness like Theresias that crazy prophet, and I opens it and they say "Jabber puts your finger somewheres on the page" and I do, and whatever it says, that's what they do. The stupid seaside hicks. So, like I said, Annie she puts her finger on the page, and you know what it says?

> *CIEL pauses on the first note of p.40. Laughter.*

UNDER A PALMTREE.

> *CIEL continues to play p.40—top of page until 40/4/1. JABBER speaks over the music.*

That was nothing to her: No meaning there: she closed the book and slept: When lo! in her dream she sees *her Enoch sitting on a height, Under a palmtree, over him the Sun:* Enoch Arden *"He is gone" she thought "he is happy, he is singing Hosanna in the Highest"* with the Lord himself in heaven. *Here she woke, Resolved, sent for* Philip *and said wildly to him*

CIEL (*sings*) *"There is no reason why we should not wed."*

JABBER *"Then for God's sake, for both our sakes, So will you wed me, let it be at once*, let's do it today" says he.

> *CIEL plays 40/5/3 last beat and all of p.41. JABBER speaks over the music.*

So these were wed and merrily rang the bells, Merrily rang the bells and they were wed. In the Anglican church St. Peter's on the Hill and Mrs Marsden made her seafood castle and her blueberry wedding cake and they danced to Vince Pottie's one-man band all night and they seemed real happy *But never merrily beat Annie's heart. A footstep seem'd to fall beside her path, She knew not whence; a whisper in her ear, She knew not what; not loved she to be left Alone at home, nor ventured out alone. often Her hand dwelt lingeringly on the latch,*

Fearing to enter: Philip thought he knew: Such doubts and fears were common to her state, but when her child was born, Then her new child was as herself renew'd, Then the new mother came about her heart, Then her good Philip was her all-in-all, And that mysterious instinct wholly died.

> *CIEL plays and sings "Morgen" by Strauss (p.53). Pause. In silence, JABBER continues.*

where was Enoch?

Enoch Arden was lost. Enoch Arden didn't know nothing of all this because he got lost on the Cape of Good Hope or whatever the hell it's called for all these 9 years ended up on one of them little bikini islands where they do nuclear testing so his brain got swizzled around and he didn't know who the hell he was so he just lay around, eatin bananas, *Soft fruitage, mighty nuts, and nourishing roots;* and making kookaburra noises, and couldn't add two and two.

> *CIEL plays an improvisation based on 43/2/1 until the dissonant chord which follows "wait" below.*

He was fried man, the two buddies he was stranded with, one died of sunstroke, the other had been hurt in the shipwreck, and he died a slow death with the broken back, right, he wasn't fifteen years old.

In those two deaths Enoch *read God's warning "wait."*

> *CIEL plays a dissonant chord.*

This was the rainforest, right?

The *winding glades high up like ways to Heaven, The slender coco's drooping crown of plumes, The lightning flash of insect and of bird, The lustre of the long convolvuluses* convolvuluses—that'd be your basic trumpet flower—*That coil'd around the stately stems, and ran Ev'n to the limit of the land, the glows And glories of the broad belt of the world, All these he saw; but what he fain had seen He could not see, the kindly human face, Nor ever hear a kindly voice, but heard The myriad shriek of wheeling ocean-fowl, The league-long roller thundering on the reef, The moving whisper of huge trees that branch'd And blossom'd in the zenith,*

down the shore he ranged, or all day long Sat often in the seaward-gazing gorge, A shipwreck'd sailor, waiting for a sail:

> *CIEL plays p.43, Andante—43/2/1 until end of p.44,*
> *repeating the last 6 bars of p.44 as necessary. JABBER speaks*
> *over the music.*

but *No sail from day to day, but every day The sunrise broken into*
scarlet shafts Among the palms and ferns and precipices; The blaze
upon the waters to the east; The blaze upon his island overhead; The
blaze upon the waters to the west; Then the great stars that globed
themselves in Heaven, the hollower-bellowing ocean, and again The
scarlet shafts of sunrise—but no sail.

BUT NO TALL SHIP NO RESCUE; NO HUMAN FACE

And he started going crazy, right? Truly mad, delirious like Linda
upstairs when Rory starts pushing her buttons and she gets out the
kitchen knife, seeing *phantoms Before him haunting him, or he*
himself Moved haunting people, known Far in a darker isle beyond the
line; The babes, their babble, Annie, the small house, The climbing
street, the mill, the leafy lanes, The horse he drove, the boat he sold, the
chill November dawns and dewy-glooming downs,

And just when he thought he would die alone on that island he
hears a talking chattering, the—chattering of men, of sailors, such
a clamour,

so he heads *Downward from his mountain gorge the long-hair'd long-*
bearded solitary, that's what they woulda called him then, that's how
people see me, when I go out on Queen Street, asking for money for
a bus ticket, putting out my hat, that's what they call me the solitary
gutter rat hardly human, he looked hardly human, just like us when
we sleep on the grates like last winter Ciel your hair all ratty your
face like leather weather-beaten your clothes ratty, your feet frozen
blocks—remember not feeling your feet when we were sleeping on
University Avenue in February and and people would pass us and it
was like they didn't see us, they didn't see us at all we were invisible,

see-through people, we were stranded on an island that's how far
away we were from them, far on a darker isle,

you know, you know? Hardly human, barely human muttering and
mumbling like Jeff, *idiotlike, it seem'd,* like me with my dkjf;alkfjas
(He talks in gibberish for five seconds.) language, *making signs They*
knew not what—that's like us, eh, we are so alone in our so called
madness we are like Enoch Arden stranded ten years on a desert

island and nobody sees who we really are, the shimmering souls that we really are.

> *CIEL plays music 45/1/1 – 45/2/1, JABBER continues.*

Well finally after food and drink and relaxation he made them understand who the hell he was that he was Enoch Arden so they were good guys, they gave him passage home, and *DULL the voyage was with long delays,* Oh my God like the time they took us all to Orlando Disneyland 4 hours in the goddamned Miami airport and *The vessel scarce sea-worthy* that's what I told the stewardess we very near crashed,

and then after months and months and months *beneath a clouded moon He like a lover down thro' all his blood*

> *CIEL plays 45/5/1, beat 4 until end of p.45.*

Drew in the dewy meadow morning-breath Of England, and *moving up the coast they landed him, Ev'n in that harbor whence he sail'd before.*

Do you believe I stood in front of St. John's finest citizens and I delivered this poem I was up there 4 and a half hours Ciel, not counting the song, nobody hardly breathed you could hear their hearts beating because you see, they were there with me, even though in actual actuality most of em took off at the hour mark even my mum and my aunt left at an hour fifteen on account of Rosalie's thrombosis but but after, after when I'm walking home, I'm thinking this IS my home, I just did something unforgettable and THIS IS MY HOME they will never forget me here, and I will always belong to this town on the sea with all the fog *LAST, as it seem'd, a great mist-blotted light Flared on him, and he came upon the place.*

> *Music starting at 46/1/1, JABBER continues over the music. CIEL should play no farther than 46/3/3.*

His heart foreshadowing all calamity, That's good Ciel, *His eyes upon the stones, he reach'd the home Where Annie lived and loved him, and his babes In those far-off seven happy years were born; But finding neither light nor murmur there crept Still downward thinking "DEAD, or DEAD to me!"*

> *CIEL stops playing.*

Kristin Mueller
photo by Steve Marsh

I went back there, Ciel, I never tol' ya, last Christmas,

I flew into Moncton Airport see, they hadn't seen me in twenty-two years Ciel since the accident because I didn't have my wallet on me so nobody called em, right? And here I was, deeply comatose for six months, friggin bilaterally decerebrated, I had severe traumatic encephalopathy dear, serious brain sickness, I was on a respirator man, 6 months, major upper brain stem injury, and look at me now, I was considered DEAD and I came back, but but I didn't get it together to get back home until last Christmas when Larry lent me the cash, right? You remember Ciel, and so I'm walking up the street, Delaney street and its just the same but not the same. And and I know, I just know they aren't there, so I get to my house, the house I grew up in and I go up the steps and I knock on the door,

And my eldest brother Dave answers. But he doesn't know me. He makes a mean face and he goes: "get the f outa here creep or I'll blow your brains out" I go "Dave it's me" And you know what he does? He calls the cops, says he's never seen me in his life I'm a stalker, I been hangin around the neighbourhood for the last six months, I tell him HEY, he's my brother—*Down to the pool and narrow wharf he went, Seeking a tavern which of old he knew,* he goes down to the pub, the local drinking hole, where else would ya go? That's where I went when they let me out, and this enormously huge fatty fat Miriam who owns the pub she was a talker, and she told him everything about the town, not havin a clue who he was, she told me all about my brother not speakin to my dad, and my cousins beatin on my uncle after he had stolen their car, she told him of the baby's death, Annie's poverty, How Philip swept in and saved the day, *his long wooing her, Her slow consent, the birth Of Philip's child: and o'er his countenance No shadow past, nor motion:* he played his cards very close to his chest you know, the way I do, but my Christ he wanted to see her again, I mean just imagine if I hadda be away from you Ciel, you are my oxygen, my breath, your music is my blood,

> *CIEL plays 45/2/2, beat 3 – 45/5/1. JABBER continues to speak over the music.*

"If I might look on her sweet face 'gain And know that she is happy." So the thought Haunted and harass'd him, and drove him forth, because I hadda see my son, *(CIEL's playing pauses.)* eh, my mum had been raisin him as her own since I left, right, I mean I was only sixteen when I got Patty pregnant, her folks were drunks, she had a temper, so Mum she took Jasper in, and and and so Miriam *(CIEL resumes playing.)* had told me exactly where they lived now, right? the very house. So late one night, Enoch, he *stole Up by the wall, behind the yew;* if anybody seen him they'd a reported him he'd a been booked for a peeping tom, just like I was—alls I was doing was looking—*and thence That which he better might have shunn'd, if griefs Like his have worse or better, Enoch saw.*

> *CIEL plays 46/4/4 – 46/6/3. JABBER speaks over the music.*

Philip, the slighted suitor of old times, Stout, rosy, with his babe across his knees; And o'er her second father stoopt a girl, A later but a loftier Annie Lee, Fair-hair'd and tall, she was playing with the baby, *And on the left hand of the hearth he saw The mother glancing often toward her babe, But turning now and then to speak with* my son, Jasper, *who stood beside her tall and strong,* he is a good looking boy, Ciel. I was proud, standing there on the ladder.

> *CIEL plays ʟangsam 49/3/3 until bottom of page, petering out (repeating 49/6/2 as needed). JABBER continues over the music.*

Now when the dead man come to life beheld His wife his wife no more, and saw the babe Hers, yet not his, upon the father's knee,

And all the warmth, the peace, the happiness, And his own children tall and beautiful, And him, that other, reigning in his place, so he's up in the yew tree, just like I was, lookin in, and he is so upset he is crying, and he knew that in one moment if they had HEARD his cry, like a *blast of doom* it *Would shatter all the happiness of the hearth.* So he goes off *like a thief,* that's all I did, and they put me in jail for it with the cockroaches and old lady killers,

> *CIEL plays music 51/3/3 – 51/6/2 (repeating the first two lines as needed). JABBER speaks over the music.*

And so he paced back toward his solitary home again, the pub, *All down the long and narrow street he went Beating it upon his weary brain,*

As tho' it were the burthen of a song, "Not to tell her, never to let her know."

BE BRAVE YOU BASTARD Be Brave you Bum Be Brave you Boring Brassy Bossy Bilious BABOON of a BASTARD BE BRAVE BE A BRAVE BEE A BRAVE BUMBLEBEE and on and on and you know what?

> *CIEL plays 50/5/1 until end of page (repeating 50/6/2 – 50/6/3 as needed), then JABBER continues.*

He was not unhappy, his resolve up bore him, and firm faith, he was doing a JEAZELY thing, a CHRISTLY thing,

and his will *beating up thro' all the bitter world, Like fountains of sweet water in the sea, Kept him a living soul.*

So he's back in the pub, and he says to Miriam, he goes "*This* Annie, *miller's wife,* does she not *fear that her first husband* might just come walkin back?" "oh yeah," says Miriam, "listen, if you could tell her you SEEN his dead body her psoriasis would just disappear, AND the cold sores, they come from stress too."

and he thought "After the Lord has call'd me, she shall know, I wait His time"

So ya know what he does?

Kristin Mueller, John Fitzgerald Jay
photo by R. Kelly Clipperton

He moves down the road about a hundred mile and started workin, what else could he do, he's pounding nails, he's sawing wood, he's choking on drywall, and every night he lies in his bed thinking of Annie and their babes. And every night there was Annie 100 miles away, in her bed thinking only of Enoch though gentle Philip slept beside her well, *a languor came Upon* Enoch, *a gentle sickness gradually Weakening the man, till he could do no more,*

He was again far in a darker isle beyond the line *he saw Death dawning on him, and the close of all.*

So one day, sick as a cat, he goes down to the pub, Miriam's there, he goes I'm gonna tell you a secret. Now swear on the Bible you will not open that big mouth of yours till I'm dead. Okay she says, done.

CIEL plays 51/3/3 – 51/6/2, repeating as necessary.

"Did ya know Enoch Arden," says he, "Sure" says she "*I knew him far away. Ay, Ay, I mind him coming down the street; Held his head high, and cared for no man, he.*" *Slowly and sadly Enoch answer'd her; "His head is low, and no man cares for him. I think I have not three days more to live.*"

"*I am the man.*"

At which the woman gave A half-incredulous, half-hysterical cry. "You Arden, you? No way. Arden was a big man" "I am bowed down with grief! Listen, if ya can stop talking for five minutes: *When you shall see* Annie, *tell her that I died loving her; And tell my daughter Annie, that my latest breath Was spent praying for her. And tell my son Jasper I died blessing him. And say to Philip that I blest him too; He never meant us any thing but good,* and there's one I will see in the after life, *(CIEL plays 52/3/1 – 52/4/4.) the puny, pretty weakly one, I loved him all the better for it* the one who *like the caged bird* flew to God— is he not yonder in the uttermost parts of the morning, yes, this curl of hair is his, *she cut it off and gave it* to me before I left, *give her this, for it may comfort her: It will moreover be a token to her, That I am he.*"

> *JABBER waits until music ends, then continues.*

Then the third night after this, While Enoch slumber'd motionless and pale, And Miriam watch'd and dozed, There came so loud a calling of the sea, That all the houses in the haven rang. He woke, he rose, he spread his arms abroad Crying with a loud voice "a sail! a sail! I am saved!"

AND CIEL YOU know what's spooky? THAT is the very dream that I had lying in St. Mike's with the decerebration going on, with all the doctors shakin their heads I am dreaming,

of the white sail, but I came back to shore.

I heard your music in my head. Calling me back to shore. I saw your lovely face and felt your hand on mine so I came back—to you...

Enoch, he kept swimming toward the sail, crying *"a sail! a sail! I am saved"*

> *We hear recorded music—52/3/1 to 52/4/4.*

and Miriam said he then *fell back and spoke no more. So past the strong heroic soul away. And when they buried him the little port Had seldom seen a costlier funeral*—they all dressed up in lace and ties and ate fancy finger food and then went home and went about their dreary lives and,

> *We hear recorded music—introduction of "Morgen" (p.53).*

Enoch seem'd to them Uncertain
as a vision or a dream,
Faint as a figure seen in early dawn
Down at the far end of an avenue,
Going we know not where

For Annie
His large grey eyes and weather-beaten face,
stayed with her forever.
That *still and sacred fire*
burned in her till her last breath.

This is the end of our story, isn't it Ciel? You and me, happily ever after on this ship in the Hope Shelter, and you know what? We don't need to leave the house again, go out on those mean streets, we can stay in this poem forever, we got everything we need here. Archie can bring us food from the kitchen, you can play piano, the little bathroom there. You and me and the ocean outside, can you hear it Ciel? Can you hear it roaring and look!!

Look at that there, that's Enoch's big boat. Will you look at that sail?

> *CIEL's recorded voice singing "Morgen" soars.*
>
> *The end.*

Tennyson's

Enoch Arden

Ein Melodrama

für Pianoforte zweihändig

von

Richard Strauss

op. 38

Ausgabe mit deutschem und engl. Text

Rob. Forberg Musikverlag

Ernst von Possart gewidmet.

Enoch Arden.

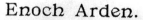

Erster Teil.
First part.

Die Textunterlage ist nach der Übersetzung
von Adolf Strodtmann. (Berlin 1886)

Vorspiel. *Prelude.*
Andante.

Richard Strauss, Op. 38.

KLAVIER.

Recitator: In langen Klippenreih'n blieb eine Schlucht
Long lines of cliff breaking have left a chasm

8 Verse bis:
(Stichwort:) grünt in einer muldenförmigen Schlucht
der Düne.

8 strophes to:
(Catchword:) Green in a cuplike hollow of the down.

5200

5200

So wurden jene Zwei vermählt und fröhlich
135 Verse bis:
Hört und nicht hört, derweil er überfließt.
(Stichwort:) Doch endlich sprach sie:

So these were wed and merrily rang the bells.
128 strophes to:
Hears and not hears, and lets it overflow.
(Catchword:) At length she spoke:

Langsam.
Enoch, du bist klug, allein trotz all' deiner Klugheit weiß ich, daß ich dein Antlitz nimmer wiederseh'.

pp

Enoch, you are wise; and yet for all your wisdom well know I that
I shall look upon your face no more.

23 Verse bis: Doch hastig nahm er jetzt
Sein Bündel, winkt' Ade und schritt von dannen.
(Kleine Pause.)

24 strophes to: but now hastily caught
his bundle, waved his hand, and went his way.
(Little pause.)

dann:
then:
Allegro appassionato.

5200

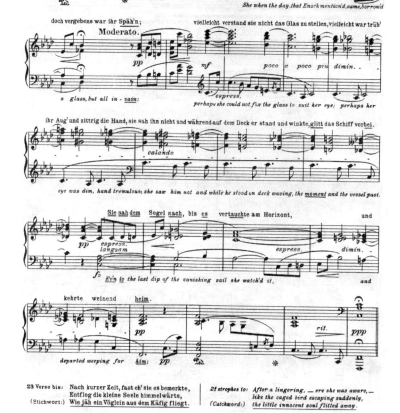

In jener Woche, da sie es begrub
85 Verse bis:
Denn unbestimmt schien Enoch wie ein Traum,
Ein Schattenbild, das man im Morgengrauen
Am Ende einer Baumallee erblickt
(Stichwort:) Und das entschwebt, der Himmel weiß wohin.

In that same week when Annie buried it,
84 strophes to:
for Enoch seem'd them uncertain as a vision or a dream,
faint as a figure seen in early dawn
dawn at the far end of an avenue,
(Catchword:) *Going me know not where.*

5200

Annie's Traum.
Annie's dream.
Langsam.

pp una corda

Und sieh! Ihr Enoch saß auf einem

etwas hervortreten

And *lo!* her *Enoch* sitting on a

Hügel, an einem Palmbaum, über ihm die Sonne.

height under a *Palmtree*, over him the *sun:*

„Tot ist er," dachte sie, „und selig singt er Hosianna in der

"He is gone," she thought, *"he is happy,* he is singing *Hosanna* in the

Höhe, dorten scheint die Sonne der Gerechtigkeit

highest yonder shining *the sun* of *righteousness,*

5200

con Ped.

So wurden diese zwei vermählt und fröhlich erklang der Hochzeitsglocken

So these were wed and merrily rang the bells, merrily rang the bells and

Schall darein.

Doch fröhlich nimmerdar schlug Annie's

they were wed.

con Ped.

But never merrily beat Annie's heart.

Herz.

Ein Schritt schien neben ihrem Pfad zu wallen, sie wußte nicht, woher; ein Flüstern hauchte

pp

espress.

A footstep seem'd to fall beside her path, she knew not whence; a whisper on her ear,

ihr in's Ohr, sie wußte nimmer was; auch war sie niemals gern allein zu Haus und wagt alleine niemals auszugehen.

Nur im Notfall repetieren!

she knew not what; nor loved she to be left alone at home, nor ventured out alone.

Was fehlt ihr doch, daß, eh' sie eintrat, oft die Hand so zögernd auf dem Türgriff weilte?

So angstvoll? u.s.w.

dimin.

ppp

What ail'd her then, that ere she enter'd, often her hand dwelt lingeringly on the latch.

fearing to enter etc

5200

(Stichwort:)
Und jene räthselhafte Ahnung starb.

(Catchword:)
And that mysterious instinct wholly died.

Ende des ersten Teils.
End of the first part.

5200

Zweiter Teil.
Second part.

Vorspiel. *Prelude.*
Allegro moderato.

Und wo war Enoch?
68 Verse bis:

*And where was Enoch?
62 strophes to:*

Wenn er am Ufer hinschritt oder taglang
Oft in der seewärts blickenden Bergschlucht saß,
Nach einem Segel spähend über's Meer;
(Stichwort:) Allein kein Schiff, kein Schiff.

*As down the shore he ranged, or all day long
Sat often in the seaward gazing gorge.
A shipwreck'd sailor, waiting for a sail
(Catchword:) No sail from day to day.*

Andante.

Wohl Tag für Tag des Sonnenaufgangs scharlachrote Pfeile zwischen

But every day the sunrise broken into scarlet shafts among the

den Palmen und Klippenreihen.   Das Glanzmeer auf den Wassern fern im Ost,   das Glutmeer auf der Insel ihm zu Häupten,

palms and ferns and precipices the blaze upon the   waters to the east, the blaze upon his island overhead;

das Glutmeer auf den Wassern fern im West, die großen Sterne dann am Himmelsdom, das hohler brüllende Meer und wiederum des

*the blaze upon the waters to the west; then the great stars that globed themselves in heavens, the hollower bellowing
ocean and again the scarlet shafts of*

Sonnenaufgangs Pfeile.   doch kein Segel.

Oft lag er dort so

sunrise.   *but no sail*

There often as he

5200

Einst hört' er auch in seinen Ohren klingen, zwar leis', doch lustig, weit, ach weit entfernt, den Schall

Once likewise, in the ringing of his ears, Tho' faintly merrily — far and far away — he heard the

der Kirchenglocken seines Dorfs.

Da sprang er auf, er wußte nicht warum, ihn

pealing of his parish bells; Then, tho' he knew not wherefore, started up,

schauderte, und als sein Blick die schöne todverhaßte Insel wiedersah — O wenn sein armes Herz sich nicht

shuddering, and when the beauteous hateful isle return'd upon him, had not his poor heart spoken

zu dem gewendet, der allgegenwärtig ist und Keinen ganz verläßt, der zu ihm spricht: gestorben wär' er da vor

with That, which being everywhere lets none, who speaks with Him, seem all alone, surely the man

Einsamkeit.

had died of solitude.

So über Enochs früh ergrauend Haar.
142 Verse bis: links vom Tisch sah er
Die Mutter oft zum Kleinen hingekehrt,
Dann wiederum mit ihrem Sohne redend,
Der groß und stark an ihrer Seite stand
(Stichwort:) Und froh zu ihren Worten schmunzelte.

Thus over Enoch's early silvering head
130 strophes to: And on the left hand of the hearth he saw
The mother glancing often toward her babe,
But turning now and then to speak with him,
her son, who stood beside her tall and strong,
(Catchword:) *And saying that which pleased him, for he smiled.*
5200

nicht der harte Kies verräterisch knirsche und längs des Zaunes sich hintastend, schlich er zur Hecken-

lest the harsh shingle should grate underfoot, and feeling all along the gardenwall, lest he should swoon and tumble

tür zurück und schloß sie so leise wie in einem Krankenzimmer; dann wankte er hinaus in's freie Feld.

and be found, crept to the gate, and open'd it, and closed, as lightly as a sick mans chamber-door, behind him, and came out upon the waste.

Dort wollt' er niederknien, doch

And there he would have knelt, but

seine Knie versagten ihm und vorwärts stürzend grub er die Finger in das feuchte Erdreich ein und betete:

that his knees were feeble, so that falling prone he dug his fingers into the wet earth and pray'd—

Es ist schwer zu tragen!
Was haben sie von dort mich weggeführt?

Too hard to bear!
Why did they take me thence?

5200

5200

Er war nicht ganz unglücklich
    70 Verse bis:
Seht eure Kinder vor dem Tode noch,
laßt sie mich holen, Arden, und sprang auf,
sie her zu bringen stracks, denn Enoch schien
(Stichwort:) unschlüssig einen Augenblick; dann sprach er:

He was not all unhappy.
    71 strophes to:
See your bairns, before you go!
Oh, let me fetch' em, Arden, and arose eager
to bring them down, for Enoch hung a
(Catchword:) moment on her words, but then replied:

Langsam.

Frau, stört mich nicht so nahe meinem Tod, laßt bis zuletzt mich meinen Vorsatz' halten.

Woman, disturb me now at the last, but let me hold my purpose till I die.

Setzt euch und hört mich an, so lange mir Kraft zum Sprechen bleibt. Ich bitte euch,

Sit down again; mak me and understand, while I have power to speak. I charge you now,

wenn ihr sie seht, so sagt ihr, daß ich starb, sie segnend, für sie betend und sie liebend; ja

when you shall see her, tell her that I died blessing her, praying for her, loving her, save

heute noch so treu sie liebend, wie damals, als wir ruhten Haupt an Haupt.

for the bar between us, loving her as when she laid her head beside my own.

5200

Und meiner Tochter Annie, die so ganz der Mutter ähnlich ist, sagt ihr, daß ich mit meinem letzten

And tell my daughter Annie, whom I saw so like her mother that my latest breath

Hauch sie segnete. Bringt meinen Segen gleichfalls meinem Sohn; und Philipp sagt, daß ich auch

was spent in blessing her and praying for her. And tell my son that I died blessing him. And say to Philipp, that I blest

ihn gesegnet, denn immer hat er's gut mit uns gemeint. Wenn meine Kinder, die mich lebend kaum

alla breve

him too; he never meant us any thing but good. But if my children care to see me dead,

gekannt, mich gern als Toten sehen möchten, so laßt sie kommen, denn ich bin ihr Vater.

who hardly knew me living, let them come, I am their father.

Sie aber darf nicht kommen, daß sie nicht mein Totenangesicht in Zukunft

But she must not come, for my dead face would vex her after life.

störe. Ach einer nur von meinem Fleisch und Blut wird mich erwarten dort in jener Welt;

Sehr langsam.

espressivo

And now there is but one of all my blood. who will embrace me in the world-to-be;

PIROL-Notendruckerei, Minden

Morgen!

poem by John Henry Mackay

Opus 27, No. 4. Composed 1894. First published 1894, Joseph Aibl Verlag, Munich. Opus 27 was presented by Strauss to Pauline de Ahna on their wedding day, September 10, 1894. Poet John Henry Mackay was born in Scotland and lived in Germany from young childhood. He was involved in a new socialist movement of art and literature which attempted to turn away from sentimental Romanticism. Regardless, Strauss used his most conventionally romantic verses for his songs. Orchestrated by Strauss in 1897. Transcribed for solo piano by Max Reger. *Original key.*

Morgen!	*Tomorrow*
Und morgen wird die Sonne wieder scheinen	*And tomorrow the sun will shine again*
Und auf dem Wege, den ich gehen werde,	*and on the path, where I shall walk,*
Wird uns, die Glücklichen, sie wieder einen	*it will again unite us, the happy ones*
Inmitten dieser sonnenatmenden Erde...	*in the midst of this sun-breathing earth...*
Und zu dem Strand, dem weiten, wogenblauen	*and to the wide, blue-waved shore,*
Werden wir still und langsam niedersteigen,	*we will quietly and slowly descend,*
Stumm werden wir uns in die Augen schauen,	*mute, we will gaze into each other's eyes,*
Und auf uns sinkt des Glückes stummes Schweigen...	*and on us sinks the muted silence of happiness...*

Son - ne wie - der schei - nen und auf dem We - ge, den ich ge - hen wer - de, wird

uns, die Glück - li - chen, sie wie - der ei - nen in - mit - ten die - ser son - nen - at - men - den

Er - de... und zu dem Strand, dem wei - ten, wo - gen - blau - en, wer - den wir

Judith Thompson is the author of *The Crackwalker, White Biting Dog, I Am Yours, Lion in the Streets, Sled, Perfect Pie, Habitat, Capture Me, Enoch Arden* and *My Pyramids.* She has written two feature films "Lost and Delirious" and "Perfect Pie" as well as television movies and radio drama. Her work has enjoyed great success internationally. She is professor of drama at the University of Guelph, and currently lives with her husband and five children in Toronto.